Cairns City Travel Guide, North Queensland Australia

Cairns Touristic Information

Author
David Mills.

Publisher:
SONITTEC LTD
College House, 2nd
Floor
17 King Edwards
Road,
Ruislip
London
HA4 7AE.

Table of Content

Summary

The world is a book and those who do not travel read only one page.

It is indeed very unfortunate that some people feel traveling is a sheer waste of time, energy and money. Some also find traveling an extremely boring activity. Nevertheless, a good majority of people across the world prefer traveling, rather than staying inside the confined spaces of their homes. They love to explore new places, meet new people, and see things that they would not find in their homelands. It is this very popular attitude that has made tourism, one of the most profitable, commercial sectors in the world.

People travel for various reasons. Some travel for work, others for fun, and some for finding mental peace. Though every person may have his/her own reason to go on a journey, it is essential to note that traveling, in itself, has some inherent advantages. For one, for some days getting away from everyday routine is a pleasant change. It not only refreshes one's body, but also mind and soul. Traveling to a distant place and doing exciting things that are not thought of otherwise, can rejuvenate a person, who then returns home, ready to take on new and more difficult challenges in life and work. It makes a person forget his worries, problems, frustrations, and fears, albeit for some time. It gives him a chance to think wisely and constructively. Traveling also helps to heal; it can mend a broken heart.

For many people, traveling is a way to attain knowledge, and perhaps, a quest to find answers to their questions. For this, many people prefer to go to faraway and isolated places. For believers, it is a search for God and to gain higher knowledge; for others, it is a search for inner peace. They might or might not find what they are looking for, but such an experience certainly enriches their lives

Introduction

The city of Cairns lies in the tropical regions of far north Queensland. For many decades it has been at the forefront of Australia's tourism industry as it provides access for several of the country's world heritage listed natural attractions. In the early days, Cairns became famous as a big game fishing destination and internationally known sports fishermen like Zane Grey and Bob Dyer made an annual pilgrimage to Cairns in an attempt to catch a world record black marlin. In those early days, local radio stations made live crosses to the game fishing fleet whenever an angler was hooked up to a "Grander" (a marlin over 1000kg). Large fish were brought back to the Cairns marlin jetty for weighing and half the town would turn out to watch.

Over the years the focus of tourism in the region has turned to eco tourism and the Great Barrier Reef and the local rainforests are now the centre of attention. Where the Cairns marlin jetty once stood is now occupied by a modern marina full of charter boats of all descriptions and overlooked by a number of modern luxury hotels. In the early days, Cairns was the major shipping port for far north Queensland and its wide streets are a relic of the days when cargo was dragged to the docks on bullock drays. The width of the streets was determined by the area needed to turn a bullock dray around. These wide streets now serve the city well as they provide excellent access for lots of traffic, tourism vehicles, plenty of parking and wide footpaths.

By far the most important tourism attraction in Cairns is its proximity to the Great Barrier Reef. It is at this point that the reef itself is closest to the mainland making access for charter boats easier. Cairns has a huge recreational scuba diving industry with several large diving schools and hundreds of charter boats. The industry caters for everyone. You may be a total novice or a highly trained professional, but you can be sure, you will find someone who runs a charter that caters to your requirements. Day trips on fast, ocean going catamarans are the most popular and these carry hundreds of tourists on each trip. This type of operation usually runs to a permanent pontoon anchored on the Great Barrier Reef, from which tourists can snorkel and dive with professional staff looking after the safety of their guests. Other services include day sailing trips to the reef and extended diving expeditions to remote reef to cater for the more adventurous certified divers.

Cairns is surrounded by rainforest. To the west of Cairns is the Atherton Tablelands and to the north is the Daintree Rainforest. You can visit all of these regions either on a day trip or by spending a few days in eco accommodation located deep in the rainforest itself. The Daintree is the most popular of these and most tours include a visit to the Cape Tribulation area and a cruise on the Daintree River to see the local crocodiles. There are several wildlife parks in the Cairns region where it is possible to see all of the local wildlife in controlled conditions. Cairns also has many other attractions and activities that are popular with tourists. The Tjapukai Aboriginal culture centre is a great place to visit and learn about the local Aboriginal people's history and culture. The Skyrail departure point is next door and this cable car will take tourists up the range to Kuranda on the Atherton Tableland. The gondolas travel at tree top level giving patrons the opportunity to experience the rainforest at canopy level. The return journey to Cairns can be on the conventional train which provides spectacular views of the Barron River and its massive waterfalls.

Cairns provides all the necessary infrastructure to make sure your holiday is superb. There is great hotel, resort and apartment corporate lodgings and relaxing accommodation, a massive ocean front swimming pool and water park complex as well as dozens of great restaurants, cafes and alfresco pubs and eateries. There are golf courses and fishing expeditions as well as fantastic shopping facilities. Cairns has an international airport and there are regular services to both Australian and international destinations. No visit to Australia is complete without some of your holiday time being spent in Cairns.

Travel Guide

Attractions

See the Great Barrier Reef
No trip to Cairns is complete without visiting the Great Barrier Reef, the world's largest coral reef system. It's made up of 3000 coral reefs, 600 continental islands and 300 coral cays. Book a day cruise with operators such as Passions of Paradise or Quicksilver Cruises to snorkel and dive among vivid coral gardens and colourful fish. Options are available to suit a range of budgets. For a longer stay, you can book a three-day liveaboard dive and snorkelling cruise with ProDive Cairns. Book a

scenic flight to get an eagle's-eye view of the Great Barrier Reef.

Get your foodie fix

Cairns has a thriving café scene, with many trendy cafés dotted along Grafton and Spence streets. Start the day with breakfast at Caffiend, a laneway café plating up dishes such as chilli eggs and French toast, with cold drip coffee and coconut lattes. Sing Sing Espresso is another popular haunt for coffee and tasty vegan treats. Tuck into wholesome salads at Silk Caffe and then indulge on its Nutella ice coffee. Take advantage of Cairns' balmy weather and dine alfresco on The Esplanade, with rustic Greek dishes from Yaya's Hellenic Kitchen and modern Asian fusion from The Raw Prawn. Mingle with the locals at Rusty's Markets (Friday to Sunday), where you can stock up on fresh local produce, including exotic fruits, dairy and seafood, from more than 180 stalls.

Learn about Aboriginal culture

Explore the rich history of the world's oldest living culture dating back more than 40,000 years at the Tjapukai Aboriginal Cultural Park. Just 20 minutes outside Cairns, the centre gives guests the opportunity to experience authentic Aboriginal and Torres Strait Islander culture through theatre, guided bush walks and didgeridoo shows. About 90 minutes north of Cairns is the Mossman Gorge Centre, an indigenous eco-tourism development that allows visitors to explore the gorge while learning about the local Kuku Yalanji culture and traditions. Travel the Bama Way, an Aboriginal journey from Cairns to north of Cooktown, and experience Queensland from a traditional perspective, from learning to throw a spear to hunting and gathering bush tucker in the mangroves.

Trek through tropical rainforest...

The World Heritage-listed Daintree Rainforest is about two hours drive north of Cairns and can be seen on a day trip from the city or over the course of two days, staying overnight in one of its wilderness lodges. The tropical rainforest is home to the most diverse range of plants and animals on earth, including the rare tree-dwelling kangaroo and the endangered cassowary. Start your day at the Daintree Discovery Centre where you can walk along the 125 metre (410 foot) long Aerial Walkway through the mid-level rainforest or take a self-guided rainforest tour. Join a gentle cruise down the Daintree River to spot wildlife in its natural habitat, including saltwater crocodiles. On foot you'll find that rainforest meets reef at Cape Tribulation, where you can easily lose hours walking through tropical lowland forest or along stretches of white sand.

...then experience it from above the canopy

The mountain village of Kuranda is tucked within the tropical rainforest, and is known for its vibrant arts community. Local markets are open daily, selling a range of jewellery, leather goods and Aboriginal art, while bookshops, galleries and boutiques line the village streets. The journey to and from Kuranda is arguably the highlight. The Skyrail Rainforest Cableway glides above the rainforest canopy then descends deep into its heart. The 90 minute experience allows time at two rainforest stations, Red Peak and Barron Falls, where you can walk among lush palm and giant ferns. On your way back to Cairns, you can travel on the historic Kuranda Scenic Railway. The two hour train journey traverses dense rainforest, winding past rugged mountains, tumbling waterfalls and the stunning Barron Gorge.

Go island hopping

Discover some of the reef's unspoiled islands from Cairns. Jump on the 45 minute high-speed ferry to reach picturesque Fitzroy Island. Here you can explore rainforest walking tracks, snorkel straight off the beach at Welcome Bay and Nudey Beach and see the beauty of the Great Barrier Reef by sea kayak. Book a day tour to Green Island, a coral cay surrounded by sugar-white beaches and sapphire waters, just 30 kilometres (19 miles) off the Cairns shore. Go off the grid at Hinchinbrook Island, Australia's largest national park island, and discover a landscape of mangrove forests, isolated beaches and sheltered bays. For a truly exclusive experience, book accommodation at reef-fringed Bedarra or Lizard islands

Tour Guide

Discover the underwater wonders of the Great Barrier Reef. Soar over the rainforest on a Skyrail

adventure and weave through the jungle past gorges and waterfalls on a historic railway. Enjoy an intimate and powerful Aboriginal experience. And kick back and savour the relaxed lifestyle in Australia's major tropical gateway.

Day 1: City, Aboriginal and adrenaline experiences

Morning

Start the day with breakfast at <u>Caffiend</u>, a laneway cafe plating up dishes such as chilli eggs and French toast, with cold drip coffee and coconut lattes. Visit nearby <u>Rusty's Markets</u> (open Friday to Sunday) for tropical fruit, gourmet bush tucker, seafood and plantation coffee and tea, as well hand-made soaps, chocolates and crafts. Get your heart pumping by zooming over a crocodile on a <u>zip-line</u> or hold a koala at the <u>Cairns Zoom and Wildlife Dome</u>. Cool off in the expansive saltwater lagoon on Cairns Esplanade, the city's social and recreational hub, before enjoying an alfresco lunch at <u>Yaya's Hellenic Kitchen</u> or <u>The Raw Prawn</u>.

Afternoon

Explore the tropical gardens, rainforest and mangrove parkland at <u>Cairns Botanic Gardens</u>. Visit its <u>Tank Arts Centre</u>, a contemporary arts facility housed in three converted World War II oil storage tanks. Alternatively, enjoy white water rafting on the Barron River, go hot air ballooning or do a <u>snorkelling</u> or sea kayaking trip to the closest island, Fitzroy, with <u>Raging Thunder Adventures</u>. More adrenaline activities include <u>bungy jumping</u> and <u>tandem skydiving</u>. Have a bush tucker inspired meal at the <u>Flame Tree Bar & Grill</u> before an evening experience at **Tjapukai**, where you'll meet the Bama Aboriginal rainforest people. They will paint your face to link you with local clans before you enjoy a corroboree dance and storytelling celebration. (Daytime offerings include boomerang, didgeridoo and spear throwing lessons, bush tucker demonstrations and dance performances.) Stay at the gracious <u>Pullman Cairns International Hotel</u> within easy walking distance of the cruise terminal and the Cairns Esplanade.

Day 2: Great Barrier Reef

Morning

The Great Barrier Reef is the world's most magical marine environment. The largest living structure on earth, it is made up of more than 400 kinds of corals and is home to 1500 species of tropical fish, plus whales, dolphins and turtles. Among the many day trips, here are three options.

<u>Ocean Spirit</u> offers a full day adventure on a stable motor catamaran to the bird sanctuary of Michaelmas Cay. Guests snorkel right off the beach, perfect for families and people who are new to snorkelling or who are not strong

swimmers. A marine biologist gives a video presentation and there is fish feeding plus the chance to take a reef tour in a semi-submersible boat. You can also try an introductory dive.

Reef Magic offers a full day trip on a fast, stable catamaran to a pontoon at Moore Reef. Activities include semi-submersible tours, glass-bottom boat tours, snorkelling, fish feeding and an onboard marine biology presentation. There's also an underwater observatory and a kids' swimming enclosure. The snorkel platform opens into a clear, shallow lagoon, perfect for beginners. As well as introductory and certified scuba dives, you can try helmet diving (in which you walk on the ocean floor without getting your head wet), guided snorkel trips and scenic helicopter flights.

Great Adventures departs Cairns on a stable catamaran for a full day or half day trip to Green

Island National Park. The closest reef destination to Cairns, Green Island is also home to a rainforest. There is something for everyone here, including snorkelling, a glass-bottom boat tour, swimming at the beach and island pool and a self-guided eco island walk. Other offerings include <u>diving</u>, parasailing, scenic helicopter flights and the Marineland Melanesia Crocodile Habitat, where you can hold a baby croc and see Australia's largest captive crocodile. You can combine this with a trip to Reef Adventures' pontoon on the Outer Reef.

Afternoon

Go shopping for local crafts at the <u>Cairns Night Markets</u> before enjoying an adventurous menu featuring native game, herbs and seafood at the contemporary <u>Ochre Restaurant</u>.

Day 3: Rainforest views and tropical seaside charm

Morning

Explore the crafts market and galleries of the mountain village of <u>Kuranda</u>, where the journey is as spectacular as the destination. The 90 minute <u>Skyrail Rainforest Cableway</u> to Kuranda glides above the rainforest canopy and descends into two rainforest stations along the way, where you can walk among palms and giant ferns. To return to Cairns, take the two hour <u>Kuranda Scenic Railway</u>, which goes across historic bridges through dense rainforest, winding past waterfalls and the stunning Barron Gorge.

Afternoon

Drive 30 minutes to nearby <u>Palm Cove</u> and have a swim in the netted enclosure or enjoy a spa treatment. Relax at one of the many alfresco cafes along the paperbark tree-lined main street, which overlooks the Coral Sea. Dine on the deck of the superb Asian fusion restaurant <u>Nu Nu</u>.

14 Day Tropical North Queensland drive

Day 1: Cairns to Port Douglas

After breakfast at <u>Caffiend</u>, one of many hip cafés along Grafton Street in Cairns, drive 68 kilometres (42 miles) north towards <u>Port Douglas</u>. Fifteen minutes out of Cairns, exit the Captain Cook Highway at Smithfield to take the <u>Skyrail Rainforest Cableway</u> for an incredible 90 minute ride over World Heritage-listed rainforest. Hop off Skyrail at the Kuranda terminal, stretch your legs with a stroll around the charming village of Kuranda and then board the historic Kuranda Scenic Railway for the 60 minute return trip to Smithfield. Back on the road, drive beside a golden chain of beaches to affluent <u>Palm Cove</u>. Hungry travellers should head to Palm Cove's award-winning Nu Nu Restaurant, which showcases Queensland seafood with a subtle Asian twist and serves lunch until 4pm. Continuing along the Cook Highway, stop halfway at Rex Lookout for magical views over the Coral Sea beaches, before reaching Port Douglas. Peruse the chic boutiques along Macrossan Street before a sunset stroll along the white sands of Four Mile Beach up to Flagstaff Hill Lookout. For a fun beachfront stay, QT Port Douglas promises one and two bedroom villas that are contemporary and quirky.

Day 2: Port Douglas

Spend the day on board a snorkelling and diving cruise off world-renowned natural wonder, the Great Barrier Reef. There are several local operators such as Calypso Reef Cruises, Quicksilver Cruises and Wavelength, each offering daily tours from Reef Marina in Port Douglas. Whichever you choose, you can expect a memorable introduction to the world's largest coral reef, home to more than 3000 individual reef systems and coral cays, plus hundreds of stunning islands with sun-soaked beaches. Underneath the water's surface though, is a kaleidoscope of coral and other aquatic life including tropical fish, dolphins, manta rays, sea turtles and giant clams, which you can swim with. After a day on the water, wine and dine amid a tropical garden at well-known Nautilus Restaurant.

Day 3: Port Douglas to Cape Tribulation

Continue north for one and a half hours along Cape Tribulation Road and explore the region's other icon, the Daintree National Park, home to the majestic Mossman Gorge. Meander through the ancient forest along the Rainforest Circuit Track, which begins at Rex Creek bridge and entails a two and a half kilometre (one and a half mile) loop with incredible views. Then book in for an afternoon Daintree River cruise through mangrove estuaries and past tropical birds and crocodiles, before continuing the drive for another hour or so to Cape Tribulation. Check into Cape Trib Beach House for the night which is set on seven acres (2.8 hectares). Here you can swim in the resort pool, get a massage on the private beach, feast at the on-site restaurant and bar and attend nightly bonfires on the beach.

Day 4: Cape Tribulation to Cooktown

Wake up with a 45 minute walk to Cape Tribulation lookout on Cape Tribulation Beach, right next to the resort. Next, drive north for an hour to see the sacred Bloomfield (Wujal Wujal) Falls with a guide, and learn about the cultural significance of this area for Aborigines. Watch out for crocodiles though, they've been known to sunbake on the nearby rocks. Venture into <u>Black Mountain National Park</u> and see the imposing mountain range of black granite boulders, stacked precariously on top of another, defying gravity. Then continue north on the Mulligan Highway for 20 minutes to historic Cooktown, and climb to the top of <u>Grassy Hill</u> in the town centre for a breathtaking view. Rest for the night at the four-star <u>Sovereign Resort Hotel</u>.

Day 5: Cooktown to Mareeba

Visit <u>James Cook Museum</u>, housed in a stunning 19th century former convent, for a look into Cooktown's remarkable history. Then 4WD west for one and a half hours to the community of Laura for a guided tour of <u>Quinkan Galleries</u>, the world's largest collection of prehistoric rock art. Begin the journey south again via the <u>Palmer River Roadhouse</u> for a late lunch and here also see rare mining memorabilia from the 1870s gold rush. Then finish the drive in Mareeba on the Atherton Tableland in time for the Reserve Twilight Safari, an experience for guests staying at the rustic Jabiru Safari Lodge. It's the best way to see the region's abundant birdlife, home to nearly half of Australia's 750 bird species.

Day 6: Mareeba to Ravenshoe

After breakfast at Australia's oldest coffee plantation, Skybury, spend the morning on a tasting tour of Mareeba's many roadside stalls, orchards and plantations. Afterwards, drive 140 kilometres (87 miles) west to the limestone Chillagoe Caves which you can explore independently or with a guide. Detour to Hallorans Hill Conservation Park and walk 40 minutes to the top of extinct volcano Hallorans Hill to see the tableland's unique mosaic landscape and geological formations. Finish the day in Ravenshoe, Queensland's highest town and spend the night at Ravenshoe Hotel.

Day 7: Ravenshoe to Undara Volcanic National Park

Follow the Kennedy Highway for five minutes west to Millstream Falls, Australia's widest single-drop waterfall, for a brief stop before spending the morning at Innot Hot Springs, relaxing in the therapeutic mineral waters that fill its six public pools. In the afternoon, drive two hours southwest to Undara Volcanic National Park, home to the remnants of the world's longest lava flow from a single volcano. Allow one and a half hours for the Kalkani Crater rim walk, which takes you up the side of a volcano and offers incredible views over the lava plains and fertile pockets of rainforest. Then sleep under the stars at Undara Experience, with permanent and powered tents that house comfortable bedding.

Day 8: Undara Volcanic National Park to Charters Towers

Continue 400 kilometres south (249 miles) to the enchanting Outback town of Charters Towers, where the heritage streetscapes hark back to the boom gold rush days of the late 19th century. Spend the afternoon just outside of town at Leahton Park, home to the largest herd of pure bred Texas Longhorn cattle in Australia. Buckle up for a Texas Longhorn Wagon Tour then explore the custom saddlery shop. Afterwards, spend the evening at the historic Civic Club, play billiards on one of two 100-year-old tables and don't forget to make a booking for their famous Friday night barbecue.

Day 9: Charters Towers to Townsville

Follow the Flinders Highway east for 125 kilometres (78 miles) before detouring to <u>Bowling Green Bay National Park</u>, home to rugged mountains, wetlands, salt pans and mangrove forests. Walk one kilometre (0.6 miles return) to <u>Alligator Creek lookout</u> for a photogenic canopy-level view of the creek, before a quick dip in the nearby swimming area. Continue to Townsville in time for lunch at <u>The Pier</u> restaurant, which serves superb seafood with sea views to match or <u>The Beet Bar</u> for superfood bowls, salads and juices that celebrate local produce. Explore <u>Reef HQ</u>, the world's largest living coral reef aquarium, which also features a turtle hospital, before whiling away the rest of the afternoon along the Strand, a palm-tree studded promenade with beaches, bars and restaurants. Later, indulge in some balmy nightlife on Flinders Street East at <u>Shaw & Co or Cactus Jack's</u>.

Day 10: Townsville to Ingham

Follow the Bruce Highway north for about an hour before taking a break in the Mount Spec section of <u>Paluma Range National Park</u>. Walk to McClellands lookout for dizzying views over the islands and coastline. Cool off at nearby Little Crystal Creek before driving the remaining 45 minutes to Ingham, a sugar cane town with a distinctly Mediterranean feel thanks to the Italian and Spanish migrants who came here at the end of the 19th century to work in the cane fields. Linger over lunch at eternal favourite <u>Casa Pasta</u> then walk off the authentic Italian fare by joining the signposted Hinchinbrook Heritage Walk, between Ingham and neighbouring Halifax. For a fittingly European-inspired stay, <u>Villa Veron</u> is a charming bed and breakfast which also hosts an Italian festival every year.

Day 11: Ingham to Cardwell

Before departing Ingham, drive west of town to see <u>Wallaman Falls</u>, Australia's highest single drop waterfall. Then it's a 20 minute drive to the coastal town of Lucinda where you can board a <u>ferry to Hinchinbrook Island</u> for the day. Australia's largest island national park is covered in mountains, fragile heathland, tropical rainforest and mangrove fringes. An island day tour takes you down the picturesque Hinchinbrook Channel before arriving at Zoe Bay on the island's southeastern side. From the beach landing, take a short walk through rainforest to the sparkling freshwater pool at the base of Zoe Falls, an idyllic swimming hole. On the way back to Lucinda, watch out for the six kilometre (four mile) sugar loading jetty, the longest in the Southern Hemisphere. Once back on land, drive 45 minutes north to Cardwell.

Day 12: Cardwell to Mission Beach

Pack a picnic and spend the morning exploring tropical <u>Tully Gorge National Park</u>. From the camping area, stroll along the Butterfly walk (it's renowned for the Ulysses butterflies that flit along this passage between September and February) through World Heritage-listed rainforest to the gorge. Tully River is popular with whitewater rafters and you can see these thrill seekers take on the rapids from Flip Wilson lookout. Continue east for an hour to Mission Beach and check into <u>Castaways Resort</u> before ditching the car for a bike and cycling along the city's foreshore, including the <u>Ulysses Link Walking Track</u>, past artworks depicting the area's Aboriginal and European history.

Day 13: Mission Beach to Innisfail

Turn off Bruce Highway to visit <u>Paronella Park</u>, a labor of love built in 1935 by Spanish immigrant

José Paronella and inspired by Catalan castles. Set on five hectares (12.4 acres) of tropical gardens beside Mena Creek, you can peruse the castle's architecture and ingenious hydroelectric system, as well as a waterfall, gardens, museum and cafe. Then drive half an hour west to the spectacular Mamu Tropical Skywalk, featuring a 350 metre (0.2 mile) elevated walkway above the treetops. Finish the day in the bustling sugar town of Innisfail.

Day 14: Innisfail to Cairns

Drive half an hour west again into Wooroonooran National Park, home to fascinating native critters such as double-eyed fig parrots and musky rat-kangaroos, as well as Mt Bartle Frere, Queensland's highest mountain. Follow the signs to Henrietta Creek Campground where you'll find the beginning of the Nandroya Falls circuit. Allow four hours to complete the walk, which takes you across the ridge between Henrietta and Douglas creeks, before winding down to the spectacular, double-tiered Nandroya Falls. Take the long track back to the campground and enjoy a rainforest dip at Douglas Creek. Back on the road, continue north along the Bruce Highway to return to Cairns, gateway to the islands, rainforest and reef of Tropical North Queensland.

15 Day Savannah drive across Northern Australia

Day 1: Cairns to Ravenshoe

From Tropical North Queensland's unofficial capital, Cairns, sandwiched between the Great Barrier Reef and the Daintree Rainforest, drive an hour west along the Captain Cook Highway to the orchards, cane fields and coffee plantations of Mareeba. Make your first stop the Skybury Café for lunch at Australia's oldest coffee plantation.

Continue 40 minutes south through the Atherton Tablelands to <u>Hallorans Hills Conservation Park</u>. Spend the afternoon following the three kilometre (two mile) return hike to the top of extinct volcano Hallorans Hill, and take in the tablelands' unique mosaic landscape. Finish the day further south in Ravenshoe, Queensland's highest town, and camp at <u>Tall Timber Motel and Caravan Park</u>.

Day 2: Ravenshoe to Georgetown

Rested and refuelled, visit Australia's widest waterfall, <u>Millstream Falls</u>, on the outskirts of town, before continuing along the Kennedy Highway. Detour 10 minutes off the highway to Innot Hot Springs and spend the morning relaxing in the therapeutic mineral waters. Back on the highway, drive 140 kilometres (87 miles) through wooded savanna grasslands to <u>Undara Volcanic National Park</u>, home to remnants of the world's longest lava flow from a single volcano. Allow 1 1/2 hours for the Kalkani Crater Rim Walk, which takes you up the side of a volcano, offering incredible views over the lava plains and pockets of rainforest. It's a further two hour drive to the centre of the Etheridge goldfield, Georgetown, where you can stay in cabins or campsites at Goldfields Caravan Park (call ahead to book).

Day 3: Georgetown to Normanton

While Georgetown's fossicking glory days may be over, you can still see the world's largest mineral collection at TerrEstrial – the Ted Elliott Mineral Collection, which has more than 4500 specimens on display. Head back on the Savannah Way and drive two hours west to the Croydon Club Hotel for a classic Aussie pub lunch (think battered fish and chips and steak sandwiches). Visit the nearby heritage-listed Croydon Cemetery, where you can still see the elegant inscriptions carved into Chinese graves, left over from the Gulf Savannah gold rush at the and of the 19th century. Then refresh with an afternoon dip in picturesque <u>Lake Belmore</u>, the largest body of fresh water in the Gulf Savannah, before hitting the road and driving the remaining two hour trip to <u>Normanton Tourist Park</u>, on the edge of the Gulf of Carpentaria.

Day 4: Normanton to Burketown

No visit to <u>Normanton</u> is complete without a photo with Krys the Savannah King in the town centre. He is an almost nine metre (30 foot) long, life-size replica of the largest crocodile ever captured, found in the nearby Norman River. After selfies, detour 45 minutes north, weaving through wetlands dotted with wading birds, to Karumba for freshly caught seafood at the Sunset Tavern on the beach. Driving back through Normanton, follow the Burketown Normanton Road west, stopping at the signposted Burke and Wills memorial – the most northerly point of the ill-fated explorers' 1861 expedition. Then continue 210 kilometres (130 miles) along dirt road to Burketown, the Gulf's oldest town, on the banks of the Albert River.

Day 5: Burketown to Hell's Gate

Spend the morning casting your line into the nearby Albert River, touted as Australia's barramundi capital. Before you set off, ask locals which fishing spots have been most successful of late (the best spots change often, depending on seasons, tides and weather). Then spend the afternoon back on the Savannah Way, driving 210 slow kilometres (130 miles) west on corrugated road to Hell's Gate Roadhouse in Nicholson, where you can stock up on food and fuel and stay in simple accommodation.

Day 6: Hell's Gate to Borroloola

Start early for the drive west along Wollogorang Road: more than 300 kilometres (186 miles) of dirt road and river crossings. Stock up on supplies before leaving, as this is one of the more secluded stretches of the Savannah Way. Travellers in the 1800s feared the area west of Hell's Gate Roadhouse, as no law was enforced after this point. Today, however, it's a scenic Outback route through golden savanna woodlands. It takes you over the border into the Northern Territory, to the friendly fishing village of Borroloola and popular McArthur River Caravan Park.

Day 7: Borroloola to Daly Waters

Half an hour south on the Carpentaria Highway, drive into Caranbirini Conservation Reserve, home to towering sandstone spires (some up to 25 metres, or 82 feet, high) known as the Lost City. Do the two kilometre (1.2 mile) Barrawulla Loop Walk through these dramatic pillars, as well as eucalypt woodland and over the Caranbirini Waterhole. Pack your binoculars and a camera: a zoo's worth of different birds can be seen around the water. Back on the highway, continue 346 kilometres (215 miles) west to the Stuart Highway intersection and spend the night at the Daly Waters Pub. Draped in bras, banknotes and other memorabilia left behind by travellers, this historic pub opened in 1938 to service passengers and crew from the nearby airfield.

Day 8: Daly Waters to Katherine

Journey two hours north on the Stuart Highway and take Martin Road to the palm-fringed Bitter Springs in Elsey National Park. It's a stunning swimming hole and quieter than nearby Mataranka thermal pool. Back in the car, continue 167 kilometres (104 miles) on the highway through Mataranka and Katherine to Nitmiluk Caravan Park, with an enviable locale right by spectacular Nitmiluk Gorge (also known as Katherine Gorge). Marvel at the gorge's towering walls while the setting sun illuminates different colours in the sandstone on the Nabilil Dreaming Sunset Dinner Cruise down the Katherine River. Along the way you'll learn about the traditional owners of this area, the Jawoyn people, while being treated to a three-course feast of fresh local produce cooked on board. Conveniently, the departure point is right by the caravan park.

Day 9: Katherine

The best way to see the Katherine region's rugged landscape, cut by deep gorges, dotted with remote waterfalls and scattered with vast cattle stations, is by air. And the best helicopter experience on which to splurge is the full day <u>Nitmiluk Ultimate Tour</u>. The tour has a maximum of three passengers. The pilot doubles as tour guide, explaining the historical and cultural significance of the landmarks below (some of which are so secluded they don't have official names). You'll visit waterfalls, see rock art and swim in a rock pool that's only helicopter accessible, making it exclusively yours. For a night of luxury, check into <u>Cicada Lodge</u> (neighbouring the caravan park in Nitmiluk National Park). It's an 18-room, five-star oasis, offering high-end facilities and authentic Aboriginal experiences.

Day 10: Katherine to Timber Creek

Return to the Stuart Highway and back through the township of Katherine before taking the Victoria

Highway 2 1/2 hours south to <u>Gregory National Park</u>, the Territory's second largest national park, covering 13,000 square kilometres (5000 square miles). It's thick with boab trees and limestone formations. Give yourself 90 minutes to follow the <u>Nawulbinbin Walk</u> from the Joe Creek picnic area. You'll pass ancient Aboriginal artwork and ascend to the base of an escarpment with breathtaking views over the lush surrounds. Then make use of the facilities at the bottom with a barbecue picnic lunch. Continue another 108 kilometres (67 miles) south to the small roadside town of Timber Creek, where you can rest your head at the grassy <u>Circle F Caravan Park and Motel</u>, after watching nightly turtle and crocodile feedings by the creek.

Day 11: Timber Creek to Kununurra

After a 225 kilometre (140 mile) drive west on the Victoria Highway, cross the border into Western

Australia and take a refreshing dip in <u>Lake Argyle</u>, Australia's second largest freshwater man-made reservoir. Follow signs to the boat ramp for the easiest access to the water's edge. Though Lake Argyle is home to freshwater crocodiles, these prehistoric creatures are timid and generally considered harmless to humans. Once you've cooled off, drive back along Lake Argyle Road to the Victoria Highway for the remaining one hour drive to the lively East Kimberley Outback town, Kununurra. Peruse the town's impressive assortment of art galleries, including <u>Artopia</u> and the <u>Artlandish Aboriginal Art Gallery</u>, before picking up a keepsake (or just window shopping) at <u>Kimberley Fine Diamonds</u>. With the <u>Argyle Diamond Mine</u>, the largest diamond producer in the world, less than 200 kilometres (124 miles) south of the city, you'll find an exquisite array of sparkling designs, including many featuring the famous pink diamonds that are only found in this area.

Day 12: Kununurra to El Questro

Continue two hours west to one of Western Australia's most famous stations, El Questro Wilderness Park. Encompassing a mammoth one million acres, this working cattle station features dramatic mountains and deep gorges, incredible thermal pools and hiking trails, three resorts including a five-star homestead, and one of the most picturesque camping grounds in the Outback, with architecturally designed amenities. Spend the afternoon doing the half day Emma Gorge Walk and Zebedee Springs tour, involving a moderately difficult hike over rocky terrain to the picture-perfect Emma Gorge, complete with waterfalls and clear swimming water. Then you'll be taken to the thermal Zebedee Springs, surrounded by palms, pandanus and fiery red cliffs.

Day 13: El Questro to Halls Creek

Drive back towards Kununurra to reach the Great Northern Highway, then follow it 250 kilometres (150 miles) south to World Heritage-listed Purnululu National Park, home of the bizarre Bungle Bungle Range. The Bungle Bungles are a maze of orange and black striped sandstone domes, like giant beehives, and you can walk through this Kimberley icon via the easy Cathedral Gorge Walk. Cathedral Gorge is a like an enormous natural amphitheatre, with the natural rock formation creating fascinating acoustics. Allow two hours to explore this area. Back on the highway, continue another 220 kilometres (137 miles) south to the old gold prospecting town of Halls Creek, where you can spend the night at the Kimberley

<u>Hotel</u>, which has a series of comfortable and well appointed rooms.

Day 14: Halls Creek to Derby

Still on the Great Northern Highway, continue 525 kilometres (326 miles) west, past Fitzroy Crossing, before detouring 40 minutes north on the Derby Highway to Derby. On the way into town, stop at the <u>Boab Prison Tree</u> – a large hollow boab used in the 1890s as a prisoner lock-up. Then pick up some homemade jerky from <u>Sampey Meats</u> to snack on while you watch King Sound's colossal tides (more than 11 metres, or 36 feet, high) from Derby Wharf, just north of the town centre. Derby has the highest tides in Australia and among the highest in the world. You might even spot crocodiles in the mangroves. Then retire to <u>Derby Lodge</u> for a contemporary, self-contained stay and impressive fare at popular <u>Neaps Bistro</u>.

Day 15: Derby to Broome

On the final leg of the Savannah Way, drive south again to rejoin the Great Northern Highway 225 kilometres (140 miles) west to <u>Broome</u>. Before reaching Broome, briefly detour north onto Broome Cape Leveque Road and the <u>Willie Creek Pearl Farm</u>, a local icon. Take the two-hour catamaran <u>eco-cruise</u> to spot local wildlife such as dolphins, dugongs and manta rays, and learn about the local pearling industry. Then follow the highway into Broome in time for a sunset <u>camel ride</u> on famous Cable Beach. It's a fittingly magical end to a bucket list road trip across Australia's north.

Cairns Holiday Accommodation

Hotels, Resorts and Apartments

Hundreds of thousands of international visitors come to north Queensland every year and stay in

Cairns accommodation. Cairns is on almost every Australian visitors radar because of its proximity to the Great Barrier Reef and the world heritage listed rainforests in the region. People from all walks of life come to Cairns to stay, during their holidays, so accommodation for all requirements is available. There are a number of popular places to stay within the Cairns region. The first of these is the Cairns CBD. Here you will find everything from dozens of backpacker lodges and hostels, apartment style resorts and international hotels. The backpacker industry in Cairns is huge as tens of thousands of young people come here to dive and snorkel on the reef and there are a multitude of dive schools together with charter boats that cater for all levels of scuba diving competency.

These hostels are located throughout the city and range from boarding house accommodation, right through to flashpackers with entertainment, huge swimming pools and barbeque areas. Most families are looking for self catering accommodation and fully managed and serviced holiday apartments are ideal for them. The Cairns esplanade is an ideal place to look for this style of accommodation. Prices on the esplanade are higher and less expensive alternatives are readily available, if you don't mind going back a street or two from the waterfront. International hotels can be found throughout the city. The higher standard, and generally, the most sought after of these, are located close to the marina precinct. Some of these are right on the waterfront and overlook the comings and goings of the Cairns charter boat industry. There are also several very popular family resorts situated a short distance from the Cairns CBD and these tend to provide a completely holistic approach to family holidays with organised activities, in house restaurants and superb family facilities.

To the north of the city are the Cairns Beaches. These comprise Machans Beach, Yorkeys Knob, Trinty Beach, Clifton Beach, Palm Cove and Ellis Beach. Many tourists like to stay here as fine resorts located right on the beachfront provide the total accommodation and relaxation package. These beach front suburbs tend to offer that boutique resort and dining atmosphere that most people find so appealing. Health spa's, golfing resorts and fully integrated luxury hotels can all be found in this region. The atmosphere here is eclectic with many alfresco restaurants and cafes set on the edge of golden beaches overlooking the Coral Sea. There are also island resorts within easy reach of Cairns. The best known of these are Green Island resort and Lizard Island resort and there are several others. These provide access to the Great

Barrier Reef as well as a five star accommodation experience. Any tourist coming to stay in Cairns will be able to find accommodation where the price is right for the standard of accommodation that is being offered.

Cairns Luxury Accommodation

Five 5 Star Boutique Accommodation - Cairns Luxe

If you like to stay in luxury accommodation, then Cairns is the place for your next holiday. Cairns is located in the far north of Queensland in the wet tropics zone that is home to some of the last tropical rainforest in the world, that is still in pristine condition as well as being the most popular jumping off point, for international tourists, wanting to visit the Great Barrier Reef. In Cairns, you will find a selection of the best luxury places to stay that you can imagine. The range is extraordinary with excellent hotels located right in the Cairns CBD or in remote locations like the Daintree Rainforest. Fantastic resorts offer exceptional accommodation and activities. For example you can stay at a golf resort in Cairns or travel to somewhere special like Green Island or Lizard Island which both have luxury resorts and are situated right on the Great Barrier Reef. Luxe self contained apartment style accommodation and superb holiday homes are also available in Cairns, along the Cairns northern beaches in places like Palm Cove and also a little further north in beautiful Port Douglas.

The Cairns CBD, with its distinctive wide streets, is situated right on the estuary from which all the Great Barrier Reef tours leave. Right along the river front, marina area and Cairns esplanade you will find the finest lodgings of all descriptions. The CBD is also filled with fabulous shopping arcades, night markets and a fantastic selection of restaurants, diners, fast food outlets and cafes. Everything you could possibly need is right at your fingertips. The Cairns CBD has no beachfront area. Just to the north of the city, places like Palm Cove, Trinity Beach, Clifton Beach and Yorky's Knob all have great beaches with lots of luxury beachfront accommodation available. The furthest from the city is Palm Cove which is only about twenty minutes drive. Port Douglas is also only a short drive to the north and it has some of the best luxe accommodation in Australia.

Your Cairns holiday should be spent enjoying the best luxury accommodation that can be found in this beautiful holiday city.

Cairns Motels - Motel Accommodation

Cairns motels have a range of products to suit every budget. From three-star to five-star plus the choice of quality products is enormous. Motels in this region have a reputation which is second to none.

Club Crocodile Hides Hotel - offers affordable Cairns Holiday Accommodation right in the city heart. Guests are usually surprised by the high quality of this 3 Star Hotel. Over the years Club Croc has achieved a deserving reputation as one of the most popular hotels in and around Cairns, perfect for families and people of all kinds.

Rydges Esplanade Resort Cairns - Centrally located on The Esplanade along the famous Cairns foreshore, Rydges Esplanade Resort Cairns welcomes guests to Australia's tropical north.

Cairns Tropical Gardens - With a central location, you'll find a large shopping centre & Cazaly's Sports Club within 100 metres of the Motel and of course all tours leave from their spectacular entrance foyer along with a local bus service if required.

Mercure Hotel Harbour side Cairns - offers an affordable and relaxed five star experience as a base for exploring beautiful Tropical North Queensland - where two unique World Heritage areas combine - the Great Barrier Reef and the ancient rainforests of the Cairns region.

Mantra Esplanade - a central location just a few steps to the yacht harbour, lively street cafes, upscale restaurants, duty free shopping, casino, and the Cairns Esplanade Swimming lagoon a seawater pool designed for kids of all ages.

These are just a few of the many fine Hotels and Motels available in Cairns, and there are some which are still being established, so no mater what your holiday itinerary requirements, there is bound to be a Cairns hotel or motel to suit you and your budget.

Cairns Resorts

Cairns resorts rank with the best in Australia. The city has a reputation globally as one of the worlds leading holiday destinations and the range of tours, attractions and accommodation is practically endless. Cairns first grew to international fame as one of the leading marlin fisheries in the world and famous fisher folk such as Zane grey and Bob Dyer visited regularly in an attempt to capture world records. The fame of the natural beauty of the area and the coral reef structures slowly grew to out shine its original attractions and today it is a Mecca for tourists from the world over.

Resorts in Cairns offer a huge range of styles and facilities. The cities esplanade is home to some of the most splendid. Such properties as BreakFree

Royal Harbour, Mantra Trilogy, Cairns resort by Outrigger, Rydges Esplanade and Tradewinds resorts are all complemented by other fabulous properties such as the Cairns International Hotel, Cairns Harbour Lights and the Sofitel Reef Casino. Family resorts like The Lakes Resort, Southern Cross Atrium, Mercure Harbourside Hotel, The Hotel Cairns and Waterfront terraces all combine to offer a stunning array of accommodation.

A holiday in Cairns is not complete without experiencing some of the great tours and attractions that are available. There is a multitude of trips and tours to the Great Barrier Reef. You can experience either day or extended dive expeditions with companies such as Sunlover Cruises, Reef Encounter, Quicksilver Tours and you can visit such wonderful destinations as Green Island, Michaelmas Cay, and the islands and reefs of the Great Barrier Reef and the Coral Sea. To the

North lies the world heritage listed Daintree Rainforest, Cooktown and Cape tribulation which are must see destinations in their own right and to the west you will find the Atherton Tableland, Kuranda, the Barron Falls and the fabulous Skyrail journey.

The city of Cairns and its surrounds will keep your holiday interest for many days and it is a fabulous family destination as well with a multitude of activities to entertain even the most difficult children. There is always something new to explore or some new place to go to keep their interest high.

In this site you will find a plethora of information to help you plan and book the right place to stay for your Resort holiday. Our helpful staff can be contacted by email or by telephone. Our phone number from overseas is +61 7 41286607 and from within Australia we have a freecall number 1800 815 378 for you to call.

Cairns Apartments

Units - Town House - Condominium

If it is room to move that you are looking for when booking your ideal place of accommodation for your next trip to Cairns, then why not check into one of the numerous Cairns Apartment properties within the city. From the CBD and the northern beaches like Palm Cove and Trinity Beach to the tranquil rainforests around Cairns, there are numerous options for you to decide between that will have you enjoying all of the main attractions that this number one holiday destination provides. All year round visitors from across the globe come to soak up the rays, laze on the pristine white sandy beaches that ribbon the coastline, visit the Great Barrier Reef and the neighbour islands and other attractions such as the Daintree Rainforest, rivers and Atherton Tablelands. From your chosen apartment that you check into, you can have all of this and so much more right on your doorstep for you to experience from the very moment you wake each morning.

Stay along the waterfront and enjoy the delights of the Cairns Esplanade each morning from your preferred apartment, stay down by the marina precinct and watch the coming and going of the many different luxury liners and boats each day from your private apartment balcony or perhaps tucking yourself away for complete privacy and seclusion appeals to you most where your own private plunge pool, surround sound, spa bath, bath robes and luxury living is just the beginning of what you will have included in your luxury apartment style range of accommodation.

Whatever your taste, style or budget there are many different apartment scattered all over Cairns for you to check into and each property boasts its own onsite facilities for you to enjoy during your stay. From an indoor heated pool, outdoor swimming pool, spa, sauna, gym room, tennis courts, games room, restaurants, pool bar and more, these and plenty more can be just some of the facilities that your chosen apartment style accommodation may provide you. You can book studio apartments, one, two and three bedroom suites perfect for large families and group bookings, executive suites, spa suites and so many of the apartments in Cairns will come fully equipped with their own kitchen, air conditioning, hairdryer, in room spa, CD and DVD player, cable TV, comfortable bedding, modern furnishings, private balcony or courtyard and more.

Simply book an apartment that is perfect for you to crash in come the end of the night where standard accommodations are more than affordable or book into a stylish and sleek apartment where you will want for nothing and may wish you never had to leave. Cairns is a popular tourist destination so always make sure you book your apartment or holiday destination well in advance so that you can be sure to get your first choice and when making your reservations enquire about any extras, specials or holiday packages where you have your meals, accommodation, airport transfers and tours all included into the one attractive holiday deal.

Your apartment in Cairns will be the ideal home away from home, so book today and experience the many treasures, hidden secretes and famous attractions that Cairns provides to all its traveller and tourists for yourself!

Cairns Activities & Attractions

There are so many fun activities to engage in while holidaying in, or visiting the tropical city of Cairns in Far North Queensland. It doesn't matter if you are a family group, a young couple on your tropical honeymoon, a businessman at a conference or you fit into some other category, Cairns has a million activities to keep you busy and entertained. Go to the movies, dine out in a sensational restaurant or café, play tennis or golf on one of the local resort courses, frolic on the beach, swim in the giant lagoon pool or take one of the sensational local tours to a world recognised destination.

The tours on offer in Cairns are recognised around the world. The Great Barrier Reef lies just offshore and is visited daily by hundreds of different tours. You can go for a day or a week depending on your choices. Snorkelling, swimming and diving enthusiasts are catered for, whatever they want to do or see. Introductory dives and certification course are prolific and qualified divers can join trips to the outer reef or live aboard nearby tours and excursions deep into the more remote regions of the Coral Sea. You can also just relax on a luxury sailing boat visiting the local reefs and attractions. Tours to the Atherton Table land or the Daintree rainforest are really popular. These activities usually occupy a full day and include lunch and you will visit all the best tourist attractions in these regions.

There are several local golf courses that will welcome visitors and provide a challenging course. If you want to see the Australian wildlife, there are several parks and zoos with excellent displays. Large crocodiles are seen at most of these as well as the cuter Australian animals like Koala and Kangaroo. The Skyrail provides an opportunity to visit the town of Kuranda on the Atherton

Tablelands. The Skyrail gondola system will carry you up the mountainside just meters above the rainforest canopy and then you return to Cairns will be on the train that travels across a spectacular bridge over the Barron River and adjacent to the magnificent Barron Falls.

Don't worry about getting bored on your holiday in Cairns as there are just too many packages,specials, deals and activities to engage in.

Best Things to Do in Cairns

Cairns is a small town of fewer than 170,000 people in the North of Queensland. Along with the Uluru in the red center of Australia, Cairns has become the quintessential location for visitors looking for that mind-blowing natural Aussie experience. Most tourists use Cairns as a base for their Great Barrier Reef and Daintree adventures. You guys know me by now, I'm adventurous and I find out the epic spots you need to see. These are my top things to do in Cairns, Australia!

Babinda Boulders

Even after considering all of the epic things to do in Cairns, the Babinda Boulders is right up there for me as one of the highlights of the trip. Surrounded by lush rainforest, the Babinda Boulders is a popular swimming hole for tourists and locals alike. The water was crystal clear and inviting. I swam to the other side of the pool and explored the rainforest, stumbling across a small family of turtles resting on a log.

This is a place you want to hang out at for at least half a day. Bring down a lunch or a picnic and really explore this gem of a spot. Make sure to beware of the current. It was so strong I had to enter at the top of the pool just to make it across in time and I am a decent swimmer! I sent the drone up just to show you guys how transparent this pool really is! Make sure you walk around the corner to check out Devil's Pool, which is next on the list below!

Devil's Pool

The crystal clear waters of Babinda Creek flow through the Boulders and eventually spill over into Devil's Pool. On the day I looked out over Devil's Pool it was carnage. I didn't even consider touching the water. It was beautiful watching the raw power of the water as it spilled down into each pool, one after another.

However, during times of less rain, the pools are actually a popular spot to jump in for a dip. There are some weird stories surrounding Devil's Pool. The story goes that there is a spirit of a woman, Oolana, at the bottom of the pool luring young men to their death. The tale originated after Oolana threw herself into the pool after being separated from her love. 17 deaths have occurred at Devil's Pool, therefore proceed with extreme caution.

Josephine Falls

One of the most remarkable things about Tropical North Queensland is that even when you aren't at the beach you can be on the beach. What I mean by this is that when you sit down along the banks and look up at the epic Josephine Falls you can sit on the sand. These sandy banks are found all throughout the rainforest and add an element of the oasis to the region.

Josephine Falls was booming on the day I visited but normally you can jump in the many different cascading pools for a refreshing dip In the crystal clear water!

Mission Beach

Halfway between Townsville and Cairns is the stunning Mission Beach. Four beach villages are linked together by 14 kilometers of golden sands. This coastline is a sunrise special, facing directly to the east and lined with palm trees need I say more. We woke up early and watched as the sun slowly rose over the ocean and finally breaking through some low cloud cover. Once the sunrise was in full swing, the palm trees shone along the coast.

There are plenty of things to do in Cairns or in the surrounding towns like Mission Beach, which is only a short drive away.

White Water Rafting on Tully River

The Tully River is one of Australia's best rafting locations and makes the perfect full-day activity for adrenaline-seekers. Grade 3-4 level rapids test your skills as your journey through the rainforest. In between the fast-paced action you can take in the stunning scenery and enjoy the wildlife action on the banks of the river. Prepare to get wet and wild as this adventure is not for the faint-hearted. You can join the white water rafting on Tully River from Cairns or Mission beach as we did. It definitely goes down as one of the top things to do in Cairns!

Great Barrier Reef Pontoon Experience

You can't visit Cairns without experiencing the Great Barrier Reef! It's literally a must when considering the things to do in Cairns! There are many ways to get out and explore the reef but one of the most popular is to take a ferry out to a huge pontoon that is loaded with all of the gear and activities. The ferry took us about 1.5 hours to reach the pontoon from Cairns. Once we were there we could choose activities such as:

✓ Snorkeling

- ✓ Scuba-diving

- ✓ Sea-Walker (crazy helmets that let you walk underwater)

- ✓ Glass bottom boat cruise

- ✓ Helicopter joy rides

- ✓ Waterslide

Included in the trip are all of the gear and an epic buffet lunch. The trip is a little short but if you have one day this is one of the best ways to visit the reef. You get about 4 hours time out on the reef but once you eat lunch and organize your activities time soon disappears. That's when you wish you had upgraded to the epic overnight stay, which I will talk about below. The pontoon experience cost about $250 AUD with Sunlover. To check out the details and availability of this pontoon experience you can click here.

Overnight stay on Great Barrier Reef Pontoon

Once 3pm rolls around all of the pontoon guests get back on the ferry and head back to Cairns. That is except of course, for those who are sleeping on the pontoon! That's right you can sleep on the Great Barrier Reef. Before you get too excited this isn't a luxury suite. You will be sleeping in a swag on the deck under the stars. I can assure you the swag was comfortable and had a thick foam mattress but it isn't for everyone. The stars were off the charts when I woke up at 3am and looked up to the sky. More stars than black. It pays to be away from those city lights.

The beauty of the overnight stay is it's just you and a few mates on a pontoon built for 100-200 people. There are no crowds or busy tourists looking for their kids. It's totally chill and you can really enjoy the reef experience at a much slower pace. I'm so stoked I got the opportunity to be out there with our chill little crew, snorkeling at our leisure. It was one of my favorite things to do in Cairns that's for sure!

Three crew members stayed on board with us and cooked great meals like barbecue and seafood for dinner. I think the moment that summed it all up for all of us was when we were sat at the table eating our bacon and eggs when a sea-turtle came up for air just yards away from us. Wow, we all thought! We are just eating breakfast while watching turtles swim on the Great Barrier Reef. You don't hear about that every day!

If you want the unique experience it actually wasn't too expensive considering the extra time you get on the reef. If you can fit it in your budget, I highly suggest opting for the overnight stay. However, the Great Barrier Reef experiences aren't super budget friendly so while this experience is a once in a lifetime, it will take a chunk out of your wallet. The overnight stay costs $499 AUD per person, which is about $400 USD. Considering it is $250 AUD for the afternoon experience it really isn't a bad deal.

Helicopter over Great Barrier Reef

From this point on our trip got next level. We had already just stayed overnight on the Great Barrier Reef. But not we were taking it one step further. We had chartered a private helicopter to take us back to Cairns. Flying over the Great Barrier Reef was the highlight of the trip for me. I love seeing things from the air, especially a reef. Often from eye-level, the glare on the ocean and the perspective doesn't give you the full idea of what the reef actually looks like. From the helicopter, we got it all. The pilot took us over a number of cayes, sections of the reef and taught us a lot about the reef we were studying below..

Rainforest Skyrail

The rainforests of north Queensland are the oldest rainforests in the world and subsequently are on the World Heritage List. This incredibly diverse ecosystem is so large it's hard to grasp while walking through the forest. The solution? The Rainforest Skyrail.

I'm a big fan of the Skyrail system. We hopped into a small cabin with a glass bottom floor, which made it easy for us to see the rainforest below. There were multiple stops along the way where we could hop off and enjoy the tree-canopy boardwalks to get a mid-level look at the rainforest. This is a really immersive experience giving you an insight into all levels of the forest with minimal work for those hike aversive adventurers.

The Rainforest Skyrail ends at the Mossman Falls, a huge waterfall and an epic way to cap off the trip. The Rainforest Skyrail experience is $77 AUD and includes a ranger-guided tour at Red Peak Station, which is one of the stops along the way.

Daintree Rainforest River Cruise

This was the most surprising activity of the trip. I thought it would be a relaxing cruise with not too much action but boy was I wrong. We hopped into our small river cruiser, grabbed a pair of binoculars and tuned into our veteran guide, Ian '*Sauce*' Worcester. Ian pretty much made the tour is good as it was with some help from the local wildlife. He has been running tours for decades, is an avid bird-watcher, photographer and has the best eyes of any human I've ever met!

The guy would spot a croc hidden deep in the mangroves as our boat was cruising past. When he returned to show us where it was we all spent five minutes trying to spot it until our eyes finally caught on. He spotted it while the boat was moving, while he was driving.. Ian is the king. As if I wasn't impressed enough he later spotted a Frogmouth, which is notoriously good at being camouflaged. He spotted this frogmouth and it honestly took me so long to find the bird even as he patiently pointed directly at it for what was an embarrassingly long couple of minutes.

I redeemed myself by spotting the only snake of the trip before eagle eyes Ian had spotted it. He begrudgingly joked if I was trying to take his job. Ian makes this cruise one of the most memorable experiences of the trip for me. He embodies what Australia is all about and genuinely enjoys each trip. His motto was something he repeated often.

Smiling from behind his wheel '30 years and never a bad trip, never a bad trip yet

Mossman Stand-Up Paddleboard Tour

The world heritage listed Daintree Rainforest is so big and so beautiful, there are never enough ways to explore this natural gem. Cruising on a stand-up paddleboard through the rainforest on the crystal clear waters has to be high up on the list. The challenging current kept us alert as we navigated our way upstream, inspecting every sandbank and Avatar tree along the route. Cruising through this beautiful scenery was one of the most relaxing things to do in Cairns!

We stopped after half an hour to eat some local fruits and have a refreshing swim. It was here that we turned back downstream, sitting and laying on our boards enjoying the serenity of the Daintree

Rainforest and appreciating the natural sounds of the environment.

Mossman Gorge Indigenous Dreamtime Walk

Roy Gibson had a dream and that was to preserve the heritage of the indigenous people of his region and to give an opportunity to his community to be involved in a positive project they could take ownership of. This dream became a reality when he acquired the land and backers helped him build the 20 million dollar Mossman Gorge Centre.

We went on a guided Dreamtime Walk through the Daintree Rainforest. Before we entered we took part in a smoke ceremony and asked for welcome and protection from the spirits. Along the way, we looked at communication rocks, medicinal plants, tools and other unique aboriginal traditions and ways of life. The Aboriginal people have some of the most resourceful and unique techniques in all areas of life that helped them to not only survive but thrive in the often harsh landscapes of Australia.

The Dreamtime Walk is a great introduction to the Aboriginal culture and how they interact with their environment.

Cape Tribulation Beach

Explore the beaches of Cape Tribulation, where the rainforest truly meets the Beach. It is the only place in the world where two world heritage sites meet head to head. The Great Barrier Reef runs right up to the Daintree Rainforest. It's a truly magical place and also a great place to base yourself for a few days of adventures such as snorkel trips and Jungle Surfing. Cape Tribulation is a must visit region when considering the best things to do in Cairns.

Cape Tribulation Great Barrier Reef Snorkel

Ocean Safari Tours took me out on what was definitely the highlight of my snorkeling in Queensland. The snorkel trip only uses a Zodiac-style boat, built for speed and transport. From Cape Tribulation, the boat zips you and 20 others out to a small caye/island. We didn't enter the island as it is a great spot for birds to hang out so better them than us!

The boat dropped us just off the caye and off we went snorkeling in the crystal clear waters of the Great Barrier Reef. Within seconds I was joined by a turtle and he didn't leave me for the next 40 epic minutes. The reef looked in great shape and our guides explained to us that yes there had been coral bleaching due to higher water temperatures but the majority of the reef is in good shape and it definitely looked awesome!

The second spot we snorkeled at was equally as amazing. I was once again joined by a turtle friend and hung out with him for the entire hour as he went about eating some sea-grass as I let him do his thing while shooting a few photos.

This short trip with Ocean Safari is a great way to snorkel the reef without the crowds of Cairns. Much more chill much more relaxing.

Jungle Surfing Zipline in Daintree Rainforest

While you are up in Cape Tribulation there is an epic little activity great for the whole family. Jungle Surfing as they call it up there is a zip-lining adventure through the canopy of the Daintree Rainforest. A slow-paced adventure which provides a little bit of adrenaline but not too much for those chickens of the group. Full harnesses an safety equipment make this a good introduction to adventure activities for kids and grandparents alike!

Thala Lodge

Thala Lodge is an eco-resort just out of Cairns. I didn't stay at the resort but a friend suggested I stop by to hang out in their epic little palm field for an hour. The lodge is supposed to be pretty impressive but the drone and I never made it past the palms. If you drone you know. Symmetrical palms from above are always going to be fun. Hanging out here is one of the lesser known things to do in Cairns, although another drone rocked up to share the airspace while I was there.

Bungee Jumping 3x Cairns

Bungee Jumping with a BMX bike from the top of a roof? Sure why not. AJ Hackett in Cairns is the ultimate hang out spot for adrenaline junkies. Only 15 minutes from the city center it's one of the best things to do in Cairns that involves hardly any driving! They have a giant swing and multiple bungee platforms to entertain you for hours. At the base of the jump is a big pool of water that dunks the jumpers head ever so slightly. Also at the base is a bar and a chill area for friends and family to watch as you take the leap of faith.

I decided to do the BMX bungee, it's the only place to do it in Australia so why not! I first had to do one regular jump and then one running jump from the ramp on the roof. The running jump was awesome and felt like a superman cliff jump. Once I graduated from the running jump the boys set me up on the BMX and off I went, rolling down the ramp before I came hurtling down to the water!

Cairns Beaches
The North Queensland beaches north of Cairns have developed into one of the regions most

popular tourist destinations. All Australian's love the beach and holiday places where they can stay on the beachfront is always the most popular. For this reason, developers have built dozens of great holiday resorts right on the esplanade at every on of the Cairns beaches. The northern most of these and probably the most popular is Palm Cove. It has a magnificent beach with its own pier from which you can go fishing or catch a tour boat to the Great Barrier Reef. Palm Cove boasts great local golf courses as well as a wildlife park, excellent shopping, cafes and restaurants. The beach is patrolled and protected by stinger nets.

Kewarra Beach lies just to the south and Kewarra Beach resort is right on the beachfront here. Clifton Beach is the next one as you travel south and while it is more residential it is still home to a number of great holiday resorts. A short trip further towards Cairns will bring you to Trinity

Beach. This is now an extremely popular tourist hideaway with many new beachfront holiday resorts. Trinity Beach also has its own shopping, cafes and restaurants and has a real tropical holiday ambience. Yorkeys Knob is one more step further south and lies just to the north of Machans Beach. Yorkeys has a fantastic marina that is always full of yachts visiting the Great Barrier Reef from overseas and southern states.

It is no more than twenty minute drive from Cairns to any of these beaches and public transport is available if you don't have your own car. The Syrail and Tjapukai attractions are both located on the north side of Cairns so they are very easy to access from the Cairns beaches region. You can also take the magnificent drive to Port Douglas where the road follows right along the coast allowing spectacular views of the Coral Sea.

The beaches north of Cairns provide a fantastic alternative for holiday makers staying in the Cairns region.

Cairns Beaches Holiday with Kids

The Northern beaches of Cairns are a great place to take the kids for a family holiday. All Australian families love to holiday at the beach and this region gives you so many options to choose from. Beachside activities and atractions include swimming, snorkelling, diving, sailing, jet skiing and kayaking. The beaches have stinger nets during the wet season to protect swimmers and most are patrolled. The great bulk of the places where you can stay in the Cairns beaches region is in apartment style resorts and these are what is preferred by mast families with kids as they are self catering which means the budget can be kept under control. The kids will still have access to a tv and most accommodation has internet access.

There are many family activities available here to keep the kids entertained for the duration of your stay. Trips to the Great Barrier Reef are a favourite with the kids as they will love to snorkel over the coral and see the brightly coloured fish. Another favourite is a four wheel drive trip to the Daintree rainforest. The kids learn all about it in school and now they can experience its majesty in person. On the way home a stop at the Mossman Gorge for a swim and a family picnic will be a real winner.

Cairns is very close by and there are many attractions to take the kids to see such as the sky rail or one of the great wildlife parks. Most children will be excited to see the local wildlife and if it happens to be a big crocodile they will like it even more. Every resort in North Queensland has a great swimming pool. Some are really more like lagoons, so your kids will be able to play in the pool as long as they like.

Some places are better than others to take the kids for a holiday and the Cairns beaches are one of the best.

Cairns Dining - Restaurants - Cafes

The city of Cairns has some of the most diverse range of dining that you will ever experience in any one place where you can sample tastes from around the world from breakfast through to dinner. Waterfront dining, city dining options, tranquil restaurants tucked away in the rainforest and dining cruises for something really different can all be looked forward to when holiday in Cairns in far north Queensland. Popular for its famous attractions such as the Great Barrier Reef and surrounding additions such as the Daintree Rainforest, Cape Tribulation and the Atherton Tablelands, Cairns Dining can also be added to the list off attractions that people love to try while they are here.

Lining the streets of the city, down by the water's edge or within a rainforest setting, are some of the different locations where you will find many options for dining out in Cairns. Breakfast, lunch and dinner can be a taste sensation with some of the country's finest chefs being based here in Cairns and serving up some of their finest works. Enjoy a hot latte in the morning in one of the many cafes, stop for a quick bite to eat at a local deli or take the kids to a family friendly restaurant in the city where you will find numerous to choose from.

With fresh local produce from the farms and from sea, quality goods and fruits that are all grown locally every meal you dine out for will be one to remember. Fine dining, family dining, pubs, taverns, tapas bars, waterfront dining and seafood buffets are just some of the different selections for you to choose from when finding the ideal restaurants in Cairns. Many of the accommodation establishments within Cairns will boast their own onsite restaurant for you to enjoy, but many will also be located closely to where ever you are checked into so that you can have a variety to choose between.

Join a sunset cruise where cheese and champagne are enjoyed, set sail for lunch cruise to remember, take a loved one out for a romantic dinner at one of the famous restaurants in the city or plan an event and function with a mouth watering menu for your guests to enjoy as many Cairns accommodation properties and larger restaurants easily accommodate any number of people for a memorable occasion. Italian, Mexican, Greek, Asian, Lebanese and Australian cuisines are just some of the options! Try crocodile, kangaroo or emu from one of the menus and finish every meal where you wish you could lick your fingers, it will be that good.

Accommodating all budgets, styles and tastes, the dining options that are available in Cairns suit all travellers, from low cost pub meals perfect for backpackers looking for cheap but tasty food through to fine dining experiences where the service and food is impeccable. Dining in Cairns is just one of the attractions that you will have to look forward to, so come and discover this far north Queensland city for yourself and find out why so many people keep coming back for more!

Cairns Scuba Diving

Padi Tuition - Great Barrier Reef Dive Trips
Cairns has been one of the worlds most sought after dive destinations for decades and is one of the Australian backpacker circuits most popular

destinations. A visit to Australia is not complete without a stopover here and experience all that the region has to offer. When you holiday in far north Queensland, you will find that you are closer to the Great Barrier Reef than when you stay in more southern regions and this makes it much easier to get to the reef itself. Water clarity is also excellent in this region and that makes the diving all the more enjoyable. This is a destination for everyone who wants to be involved in scuba diving. Cairns has several dive schools that have excellent facilities. Some operators concentrate on the day market and take people to the reef and back on their own vessels. Some cater for the local extended tour market and offer two, three and four night extended diving charters while others take larger vessels deep into the outer reefs of the Coral Sea to dive in remote and pristine locations.

Some of the best diving operators in the area include Deep Sea Divers Den, Reef Encounter, Mike Ball Dive Expeditions, ProDive, Sunlover Cruises, Quicksilver, Calypso charters and Haba dive. The corals here are without parity in the world so come and spend your diving dollar in Cairns.

The Cairns hinterland also provides some spectacular sightseeing so when your dive adventure is over spend a few days in some of the best places to stay in north Queensland and experience the rainforest or some of the world heritage listed tourist destinations in the area. A trip on the skyrail to Kuranda and return via the Barron Falls is one of the most spectacular trips money can buy and the Daintree Rainforest is only a short drive north from port Douglas. There are many reasons to come to Cairns for a holiday, but for those whoe love nature and the water, a Cairns diving holiday is unforgettable. During the low and shoulder seasons you will often be able to find the best holiday specials that are offered by the local diving operators and these help them fill boats with lower prices on their diving trips.

Cairns Fishing Charters

With the surrounding rivers and estuaries and fringed by some of the best ocean waters in the country, it is no wonder why so many avid fishermen are drawn to Cairns to set out on one of the many fishing charters that you can book onto that will have you fishing in no time at all. Of the Cairns fishing charters that you can book onto are purpose built vessel providing everything that you will need for an enjoyable time out on the water whether it be just for the day or perhaps overnight or even longer. Fishing off Cairns or simply from the beach or rock walls will have you eating seafood for dinner!

There are many different fishing charters that you can select from depending on how long you wish to travel out for and how much you wish to spend. From affordable day rates perfect for family outings through to fully equipped fishing boats complete with private sleeping quarters, hot showers, toilets, plasma TV and so much more. The local crew will take you to great fishing locations and have an excellent knowledge of the ocean waters and where to catch a great feed! You can book deep sea, sport fishing charters or make your way to quieter estuaries where fresh water fishing charters and fly fishing can be enjoyed.

With bait, tackle, rods and reels being just some of the inclusions that all of the fishing charters provide all you will need to bring is yourself and plenty of sunscreen. Be picked up directly from your front door of your accommodation and then be returned come the end of the day, have your catches filleted and cleaned for you and kept on ice until your return back to shore! Every fishing charter boasts little inclusions to entice you to travel with them, you just have to decide which one suites you and your budget the best.

Go fishing for coral trout on the Great Barrier Reef, or game fish for the famous marlin that can be found in these waters, tackle up to land yourself a barramundi up one of the creeks or fish the tidal estuaries for some Queenfish or many other fish species. Reef Fishing, game, sport, live aboard fishing charters and deep sea offshore fishing charters are just some of the different selections for you to choose between when finding the ideal fishing charter that is right for you. Soak up the glorious sun, reel in some great catches and have a fishing experience that you will never forget!

Most days in Cairns are ideal for fishing as it is blessed year round with some of the best conditions so book your ideal fishing charter for your Cairns Fishing. The professional staff and crew intend on giving the best time imaginable out on the water and the purpose built boats leave nothing to chance, with safety, comfort ability and little extras all being included. Whether it is your first time or not, every time travelling with any of the fishing charters that depart from Cairns will be an adventure that you will wish never had to come to an end.

Fishing is one of the biggest attractions for Cairns, so be sure to book your preferred fishing charter so you don't miss out on a seat and get on board!

Cairns Golf

A Golf holiday in the Cairns region will be long remembered for the great weather, the Quality of the courses played, the fantastic tropical surroundings and quality resort style holiday destinations. There are a number of courses where you can play and some are a real test of your ability. If you come to Cairns for a golf holiday then you should play in both Cairns, Palm Cove and nearby Port Douglas. All have a choice of fine courses, each with its own special style.

The Cairns city course is a public course of 6115 meters and with full facilities. It is located around 7 kilometers from the center of town towards the west. Water hazards are a feature of this course as the terrain is fairly flat. Half Moon Bay tennis and GolfClub at Yorkeys Knob offers a sand based all weather 18 hole course that features plenty of water hazards and is 5200 meters in length. There are two courses at Palm Cove. The Novotel Rockford resort has a 9 hole par three course which is great to give you a bit of exercise and wont break the bank, while just down the road is the best course in the entire district. The Paradise Palms layout is ranked in the top 25 courses in Australia and comes complete with excellent resort style holiday accommodation. This is a championship course set among the tropical rainforest. It is a par 72 course of 6592 meters.

Port Douglas is a resort town about one hours drive north of Cairns along one of Australia's most spectacular coastal roads. Far North Queensland is the home of two excellent resort golf courses, both of which are of top standard. The Sheraton Mirage course has in the past been the home of the "skins" game in Australia with players like Jack Nicklaus and Greg Norman both playing here. It is a Peter Thomson designed course and contains six par 3's, six par 4's and six par 5's. Not far away is the Sea Temple holiday spa golf course. This is a fine links style course with excellent facilities and some really challenging holes. It is 6261 meters in length.

In the nearby hinterland, towns like Mossman and Mareeba have public courses that welcome visitors and each has its own special charm. All of these combined, make a Cairns golf holiday a varied and exciting possibility.

Cairns Holiday with Kids

Take your kids to Cairns for their next holidays so they can share in the fabulous attractions and activities that only Cairns has to offer. Cairns is the largest tourist city in North Queensland and is home to Australia's underwater diving and snorkel industry. Cairns is located closer to the Great Barrier Reef than any other city in Queensland and has many options available to explore its beauty. Cairns is also the center of the rainforests of the tropical north and is an ideal location to base yourself with the kids so that you can journey out into the hinterland to see all that the region has to offer. Cairns also has many other activities to enjoy such as the Skyrail journey to Kuranda or the Tjapukai aboriginal attraction.

Many of the places where you can stay are largely made up from apartment style resorts that make the ideal base for a family on holidays. Not only can the parents have the privacy of their own room, but kids can be put to bed early if required. The Cairns CBD is located at the entrance to a river estuary and although the waterfront area does not have a beach as such, the council has constructed one of the largest lagoon swimming pools that you will ever see. It is right on the esplanade and only walking distance from most of the best accommodation.

The Cairns marina is also only walking distance from the esplanade so you can go on a tour to the reef or to nearby Green Island. If you bring your own car or you choose to hire a car from Cairns you will be able to see the magnificent hinterland at your leisure. The kids will love a day spent on the Atherton Tablelands visiting the spectacular rainforests or having a picnic in glorious surroundings in place like Lake Eacham. To the north lie the Cairns Beaches and Port Douglas and if you wish it is an easy days ride to visit the Daintree rainforests. To the south you can visit Mission Beach and Tully or take a day away to see Paronnella Park.

Your kids will be so excited when you tell them they are going to Cairns for their next holidays.

Cairns Honeymoon and Weddings

Cairns is a wonderful destination for anyone planning a honeymoon. Not only is there fantastic and romantic wedding night love nest for your special night, but there are a hundred and one things to do on the days that follow. You can fly in direct from anywhere in Australia and from a host of international destinations as well and you can also enjoy a Cairns wedding if that is your desire. Honeymooners, coming to Cairns will not be disappointed. You can choose to stay in an international five star hotel, a quiet resort in the rainforest, and idyllic island retreat or a beautiful beachfront resort with fantastic individual bures. All of this is here and waiting for you to investigate and book.

Many of the resorts around Cairns offer a full wedding service that includes a chapel or garden setting for the service, dining facilities for the reception and superb accommodation for the wedding night. The ensuing honeymoon will become a feature of the whole event. Many of these resorts also include a dedicated wedding planner to make sure that everything goes according to plan and nothing is forgotten. Most honeymooners will want to see some of their surroundings during their stay and many interesting local excursions and activities are on offer. A day trip to the Great Barrier Reef or the sensational Daintree rainforest will be on everyone's agenda. If you want to hire a car during your stay then the whole Atherton Tableland and Mission Beach areas as well as Port Douglas are all within easy reach and you can make them part of your Cairns honeymoon as well.

Cairns has so much to offer that your honeymoon is assured of success.

Cairns Weddings

Cairns Honeymoons - Receptions and Venues

If you are planning a wedding in Cairns or in the nearby region then get in touch with one of our consultants if you have any questions that you need answers for. Cairns is a fantastic wedding destination because it offers so many picturesque locations for you ceremony, loads of fantastic reception destinations and heaps of top class places to stay for the guests plus that special hidden place for your honeymoon. Cairns can also offer plenty of choices when it comes to celebrants, flowers, hair and beauty treatments and all of the other accouterments you will need on your special day. Cairns is also really east to get to as you can fly in direct from all southern cities as well as from overseas through the Cairns international airport.

Group rates are often available so if you are bringing a family and friends for the festivity's then some special rates may apply at some resorts and hotels. The best resort destinations come in all shapes and sizes and there will be something to suit all different budgets. The esplanade is home to many fabulous resorts and hotels, many of which also have reception facilities and many also have dedicated wedding planners and contacts for Cairns wedding photography, to assist you with all the detailed arrangements that make for a trouble free wedding day. The Northern beaches area also has lots of fabulous resorts. Trinity Beach, Clifton Beach and Palm Cove are also very popular wedding destinations in their own right as is Port Douglas. Some of the North Queensland islands like Lizard Island and Dunk Island are accessed from Cairns and these may also become part of the equation.

If you choose Cairns as your wedding destination then your honeymoon choices are also increased with many nearby Island resorts within easy reach.

Palm Cove

One of north Queenslands most popular tourist destinations is the seaside resort town at Palm Cove. The magnificent beach, which has been rated in the top ten beaches in the world is a major attraction. Palm Cove has a cosmopolitan atmosphere that is enhanced by its seaside location, colourful resorts, alfresco dining and lifestyle, all complimented by modern quality places to stay which is presented in a multitude of excellent resorts. Palm Cove is one of the northern beachfront suburbs of Cairns and is about twenty minutes drive north from the Cairns CBD. As a suburb of a large city, there is lots of shopping and the tourist attractions that are available in the immediate vicinty are fantastic. To the north of Palm Cove is the holiday town of Port Douglas and the two are connected by a sensational coastal highway where the views rival some of the most spectacular stretches of road anywhere in the world.

Some of Australia's most important tourist attractions are within easy reach of Palm Cove.The best known of these is the Great Barrier Reef. This stretch of far north Queensland coastline between Cairns and Port Douglas and incorporating Palm Cove is the closest stretch of coast to the Great Barrier Reef itself. A multitude of tour options are available from Palm Cove to visit the reef itself. Many day tours can be used, one of which departs from the Palm Cove jetty. Diving and snorkeling trips, dive tuition and training, with accreditation, are all available. The north Queensland region is also famous for its rainforests and the best known of these is the Daintree rainforest. Beautiful rainforests and lakes also exist on the nearby Atherton Tablelands which are less than an hours drive from Palm Cove. Just to the south of Palm Cove you will find the Tjapukai Aboriginal display which provides a fantastic isight into the Aboriginal culture and there is also the Skyrail which features a cablecar style gondola ride accross the treetops and the rainforest canopy, up the side of the Great Dividing Range and terminating in the coulourful village of Kuranda at the top of the range itself. Most patrons of the Skyrail return to Cairns on the conventional rail service which features a spectacular railbridge accross the Barron River just below the might Barron Falls.

The Palm Cove Esplanade is the tourism focal point. On its inshore side is a row of superb resorts, most of which are in the four or five star category. They all feature hotel style or apartment style accommodation with wide balconies that take in the view of the Coral Sea and allow the balmy trade winds to cool there interiors. Most of these resorts have alfresco restaurants set among the gigantic and ancient Melaeleuka trees that line the streetfront. At night, flares and candles light the holiday surroundings of these eateries adding to the wonderful holiday ambience that Palm Cove exudes. On the beach side of the street are holiday equipment hire services including paddle ski's, jet ski's and sail boats. All of these features make Palm Cove the most attractive tourist destination in Far North Queensland.

Palm Cove Holiday Accommodation

Of all the beachside suburbs north of Cairns, Palm Cove is the most popular and has by far the best accommodation. Palm Cove is about twenty minutes drive north from the Cairns airport and located on the best beach in far north Queensland. The superb beach is one of the many things that attract holidaymakers to stay in Palm Cove. The beach is complimented by equipment hire services that include jet ski's, kayaks, paddle ski's and wind surfers. The town has a long esplanade which is lined with coconut palms, massive Melaleuka trees and beautiful accommodation resorts, most of which command panoramic views over the sand and the Coral Sea. Most of the resorts have their own alfresco restaurants which results in a boulevard where people can enjoy the tropical climate to the full while at the same time being part of the cosmopolitan ambience that pervades throughout Palm Cove.

Most Palm Cove accommodation is in apartment style resorts or in hotel style accommodation. In most cases, Palm Cove accommodation and Trinity Beach Accommodation caters to the more affluent end of the market and most of the local resorts are either four or five star rated. The resorts are almost all built surrounding a lagoon style swimming pool as the climate dictates swimming and sun baking as the most popular pastimes for holiday makers. Patrons tend to be of international origin or have come from Australia's southern states. This migration occurs most commonly during the winter months as southerners try to escape from the winter cold. During the southern winter months and through the spring Palm Cove is alive with tourists and the accommodation houses are full to overflowing. At this time of the year it is essential to book your accommodation well in advance.

One of the reasons Palm Cove is so popular is the fact that is located within easy reach of many of the region's best tourist attractions. All the resort have a tour desk to assist patrons to take tours to as many of these as possible. All tours in the district will pick up from your chosen accommodation and drop you back there at the end of the day. Port Douglas to the north, the Daintree rainforest, Mossman, the city of Cairns, the Skyrail and Tjapukai Aboriginal display are major land based attractions. The most important attraction to see while in the Palm Cove region is obviously the Great Barrier Reef.

Tours to the Great Barrier Reef are available from either the Palm Cove jetty itself, Port Douglas or Cairns. There are hundreds of alternatives to choose from. Day or extended trips, diving, snorkeling and dive training and accreditation are all available while staying in Palm Cove accommodation.

Agincourt Beachfront Apartments
4 Star Esplanade Apartments at Clifton beach

Agincourt Beachfront Apartments front onto beautiful Clifton beach in the cairns northern beaches region. The apartments are of a four star standard and are about 20 minutes drive from the center of cairns. Palm Cove Beach lies just to the north..

When it comes to relaxing and enjoying the tropics, Agincourt offers every chance to unwind. Stroll along the white sandy beach to nearby Palm Cove or Kewarra Beach. Swim in the Coral Sea right at your door or you may prefer to relax by our large salt water lap pool. The gardens at Agincourt are a lush and tropical sanctuary for a wide selection of birds, parrots and home to the Cairns Birdwing Butterflies.

Garden lovers will delight in the colourful range of local and exotic orchids growing naturally on the rainforest palm trees. And when the mood takes you, enjoy a cool drink or cook a steak on our free gas barbecue under cover in the spacious pool side Cabana.

Accommodation Information:

Agincourt is a resort style complex of 45 luxury one bedroom apartments on a large beachfront site at Clifton Beach considered Cairns' most beautiful beach. Every Agincourt apartment is beautifully appointed. Large living areas are finished in cool white satin tiles which lead onto your own spacious private balcony overlooking a tropical beach with coconut palms or our lush tropical gardens and 20 metre lap pool.

The apartments are situated in two buildings and for your convenience both buildings are serviced by lifts. Premium linen and ironing facilities are included. Each apartment has a queen size bed in the bedroom and a double sofa divan in the living room. There is a maximum of 3 persons allowed in each of the apartments which are serviced weekly or by arrangement. Ceiling fans are fitted throughout all apartments, a colour television in the living room and your bathroom has a washing machine, dryer and hair dryer. All apartments are air-conditioned and equipped with self catering facilities so you have everything you need in the kitchen which includes a microwave, oven and cook top.

Alassio Palm Cove

4 Star Beachfront Apartment
Accommodation - Williams Esplanade
139 Williams Esplanade, Palm Cove
Alassio Palm Cove offers luxurious studios and 1, 2 & 3 bedroom apartments right along the beautiful beach of Palm Cove. This resort has a Mediterranean design and is surrounded by tropical gardens and palm trees which gives it a feel of a tropical paradise. The resort is only a

short walk to shops, bistros, restaurants and bars in Palm Cove, including many water sports and other beach activities.

Palm Cove is only 25 km from Cairns City and Airport, close to shops, restaurants & cafés and any tours & cruises you wish to experience while on holiday.

Accommodation Information:
All apartments face north or east with private balconies with all interior spaces being air conditioned. Their boutique accommodation offers studios, one, two and three bedroom apartments facing the beachfront or the free-form swimming pool. Ground floor apartments with disabled facilities are available upon request.

Angsana Resort and Spa

Five Star Luxury beachfront resort - Day Spa - Restaurant.

1 Veivers Rd, Palm Cove
Angsana Resort & Spa, Great Barrier Reef has an absolute beachfront position in Palm Cove, with fantastic Coral Sea and Palm Cove beach views. Angsana offers 5-star luxurious Suites with a chic and contemporary style promising a private retreat and carefree getaway experience.

There are plenty of activities either around the resort, within palm Cove or on a tour arranged for you by the tour staff at the resort. Palm Cove is an eclectic destination with chic cafes and boutiques, great beach activities and the region includes the fantastic Daintree Rainforest region, Port Douglas and the incredible beauty of diving and snorkeling on the reef itself.

Dining
Angsana Resort has Alfresco indoor dining and BBQ outdoor dining. Far Horizon Restaurant & Bar offers an international Alfrecso cuisine with local

seafood. The BBQ dining is set amongst the palm trees and offers beef, Kangaroo and fresh local seafood.

Lounges

There are the Ulysses & Lobby Lounge, both offer a relax atmosphere, you can laze away with a good book, play a game of monopoly or use the Wireless Internet to stay in touch with friends and family.

Spa

Angsana Spa Great Barrier Reef, a multiple award-winning Spa, is an oasis for guests to experience an extensive selection of unique treatments. Set against a backdrop of Coral Ocean at the fringe of pristine beaches, the Spa is a true retreat for one to shed the cares of the world and re-discover sensory pleasures.

Business, Functions & Weddings

Angsana has conference and board rooms facilities ideal for all types of gatherings, from business, functions, weddings, anniversaries, theme nights and birthday parties.

Angsana has a Wedding Chapel, a wonderfull & tranquil place to exchange your wedding vows. The Angsana Wedding Coordinator can arrange all your wedding plans to make you special day hassle free.

Accommodation Information:
Angsana Resort has 67 suites, they range in spacious one, two and three bedrooms. The suites have floor-to-ceiling glass doors that open onto wide patios and the tropical gardens. Angsana also has a luxurious suite, named "Angsana Suite" which comes with a private swimming pool, sun terrace and barbecue.

Ellis Beach Bungalows

Family Holiday Accommodation - Beachfront - 3 Star +
Captain Cook Hwy, Ellis Beach

The Ellis beach Bungalows are located on one of North Queensland's most picturesque coconut palm fringed beaches located just north of Palm Cove, There is nothing quite like staying in a cabin where you can just walk out the door onto a tropic al beach and laze the day away..

Accommodation Information:
Imagine waking up to the magic of a tropical sunrise, walking along the crystal clear waters of the Coral Sea and coming back to your original Aussie breakfast barbecue. The Oceanfront Bungalows offer you these delights, and all the facilities you'd expect on a tropical beachfront holiday, including a large shaded swimming pool.

Bungalow Features:

- ✓ Private Bathrooms
- ✓ One & two bedroom suitable for couples or families

- ✓ Verandahs overlooking the Coral Sea

- ✓ Queen size beds / doubles & bunks

- ✓ Colour television

- ✓ Air conditioning & ceiling fans

- ✓ Full size stove/oven & hot plates

- ✓ Microwave oven full size fridge/freezer

- ✓ Cutlery, crockery, cooking utensils

- ✓ Linen and towels

- ✓ Weekly service

Elysium Apartments

26 Veivers Rd, Palm Cove

The word "Elysium" means 'place of perfect happiness and in Palm Cove, that is what you will find as a holiday destination. Elysium Apartments is quality luxurious holiday living that combines high style and practical choices for discerning holidaymakers.

Elysium Apartments are located on Vievers Road, just a short stroll to the beautiful beach. The reost features twenty one, two and three bedroom apartments, each with its own balcony..

From privacy and security to thoughtfully planned outdoor entertaining areas, parking access and the latest IT facilities, you'll want for nothing during your vacation at Elysium.

Grand Chancellor Palm Cove
[formerly Novotel] - Four Star Palm Cove resort - Conference - Restaurant
Coral Coast Dr, Palm Cove

Grand Chancellor Palm Cove can be found just back from the Palm Cove beachfront and surrounding the local golf course. Grand Chancellor is a large resort with 245 rooms, several swimming pools, tennis courts, golf restaurants and cafes not to mention excellent conference rooms.

Located throughout the resort are 7 tropical setting pools including 25m lap pool. Each accommodation area has there own tropical pool so you can always find seclusion by the poolside relaxing in a sun lounge or having a refreshing swim. The main Resort pool is designed around rockery and waterfalls with a spa, children's wading pool and crocodile slide all covered by shade sails. The main pool offers all day poolside service ensuring a tempting cocktail or light snack is never too far away.

Not only is the Grand Chancellor Palm Cove a sensational place to holiday for adults, the activities designed for children make it a special experience for the whole family. So everyone can enjoy time for themselves and together.

Dining

Canecutters Restaurant:

Canecutters Restaurant is open 7 days for breakfast and dinner. They offer a-la-carte and the ever popular seafood buffet on Friday and Saturday nights.

Located in the Nautilus accommodation block, and next to the Reception desk and main pool, Canecutters Restaurant is open 7 days a week for breakfast and dinner.

Breakfast: 6.30 – 10.30am

Dinner: 5.30 – 9.00pm

V Dining:

Tempt your taste buds from the V-Dining Alfresco menu and sample some enticing modern cuisine with a soft candle lit dinner or relaxed poolside lunch.

Located in the Nautilus accommodation block, and next to the Reception desk and main pool, V-

Dining is open 7 days a week for alfresco lunch and a-la-carte dinner.

Open Times: 11.00am – 10.00pm

V BAR:

Relax in a cosy wicker chair at V-Bar overlooking the pool, while sipping on an exotic cocktail or favourite beverage.

Located in the Nautilus accommodation block, and next to the Reception desk and main pool, V-Bar is open 7 days a week from 11.00am till late.

Meetings

Service & Facilities:

Grand Chancellor Palm Cove has an abundance of resort facilities and services including numerous pools, recreation centre, nine-hole golf course, salon and beauty, resort shop, restaurants and bar set amidst the idyllic location of Palm Cove.

Grand Chancellor Palm Cove, in conjunction with an on-site technical team, a creative theming company and the latest audio-visual technology, can provide all the elements to create the exact meeting or event that you desire.

Team Building, Tours & Activities:

Grand Chancellor Palm Cove offers an amazing choice of activities and team building options to suit your needs including construction games, problem solving, artistic challenges, beach Olympics, extreme rafting, kayaking, climbing and orienteering to cultural activities....limited only by imagination.

Activities

9 Hole Par 3 Golf - Palm Cove Country Club

The Palm Cove Country Club is great for entertaining corporate guests or travelers alike. Their 9 hole par 3 golf course offers a stunning setting and is ideal for social rounds or Corporate events. The course is surrounded by lush landscape and spectacular mountains to make it a delight to play on. Their professional staff at Palm Cove Country Club will take care of all your requirements to ensure that the day is enjoyable and successful.

Skin Beauty & Hairdressing

The my skin beauty and hairdressing Salon is a perfect way to relax after a day of exploring the attractions in and around Cairns. They offer massage, facials, hair treatments and aromatherapy.

Weddings

Grand Chancellor Palm Cove provides the ideal setting for your special day. Located in the idyllic tropical serenity that is Palm Cove, Tropical North Queensland, the possibilities to make your special day just perfect are endless. The services and facilities of this fully integrated resort enables you with the ability to conduct all your wedding requirements in one truly unique location.

Their specialised wedding coordinator will be with you every step of the way providing you assistance, support and recommendations to ensure that your perfect day is just that.....perfect.

Accommodation Information:

The Grand Chancellor Palm Cove offers a choice of modern and spacious rooms, suites, and self contained apartments, all designed for natural living. The Superior Rooms and Executive Suites are stylish and comfortable ideal for a small family, a couple, or conference delegates. The 2 Bedroom Apartments are designed for larger families or groups, with the 2 Bedroom Apartments also featuring kitchen and laundry facilities.

- ✓ Room Features

- ✓ Tea & coffee making facilities

- ✓ Mini Fridge

- ✓ Hair Dryer

- ✓ Television with Austar (excluding 2 Bedroom Apartments)

- ✓ Shower over Bath

- ✓ Iron & ironing board

- ✓ Dry cleaning available

- ✓ Air conditioning

- ✓ Balcony or terrace

- ✓ In room safe (except 2 Bedroom Apartments)

- ✓ Wireless broadband Internet

Superior Rooms:

The Superior Rooms are ideal for small families and conference delegates. The room consists of two double beds in a combined lounge and dining area. The maximum sleeping capacity is 2 adults and 2 children.

Executive Suites:

The Executive Suites are ideal for small families, a couple, or conference delegates. The suite consists of one Queen, or 1 King/2 King Single beds in the main bedroom. There is a separate lounge and dining area with a double sofa bed. The maximum sleeping capacity is 2 adults and 2 children.

2 Bedroom Apartments:

The 2 Bedroom Apartments are ideal for families who require full kitchen and laundry facilities. There are two bedrooms, one with a Queen Bed and the second with 1 King/2 King Single beds. The maximum sleeping capacity is 3 adults and 1 child.

*Sleeps max up to a family of 5

Palm Cove Luxury Accommodation

Palm Cove is a great holiday destination where luxury accommodation lines the beachfront. This is one place where the resort developers have let their imagination run riot when designing new and spectacular resorts to compliment the beautiful tropical surroundings that are prevalent in Palm Cove. This is such apopular resort destination that many new resorts have sprung up over the past few years and the beach in Palm Cove is the best in the whole Cairns to Port Douglas region. Palm Cove is also centrally located in Far North Queensland so the tours and attractions of the whole region are available for holiday makers staying in Palm Cove.

Some of the best luxe resorts in Palm Cove are comparable with the best accommodation in Port Douglas or Cairns. The Sea Temple Resort has an absolute beach frontage position. Huge swimming pools and thatched shade huts and dining facilities surround it. The apartments are set in a U shape facing the ocean with the best luxury apartments all overlooking the pool and the view. Angsana Resort, although older, is also right on the beachfront and provides luxury accommodation.

The main esplanade then follows the beachfront and a number of luxury resorts have been built here. Although they have the road between the resorts and the beach the settings and the ocean views are all exceptional. Palm Cove is known for the huge Melaleuca trees that grow right along the beachfront. Some of these resorts include the Grand Mercure Rochford Esplanade Apartments, Peppers Beachclub and Spa, Sanctuary Resort, The Sebel Reef house and Spa, Paradise on the Beach apartments and Mantra Amphora Resort.

In the streets behind the beach other luxury accommodation can be found at Novotel Rochford

Palm Cove, Palm Cove Tropic Apartments, Oasis Palm Cove and Elysium Apartments. As you can see there is plenty of luxury accommodation to choose from and all within walking distance of the beach, restaurants and cafes.

If you are pining for a fantastic holiday being pampered in luxury accommodation, then Palm Cove luxe could be the right destination for you.

Palm Cove Activities & Attractions

Palm Cove is close to all the best holiday activitiesand attractions in Far North Queensland. Everyone wants to stay in a holiday destination where there are plenty of attraction and activities so that the whole family is kept occupied for the duration of their stay. Palm Cove is a seaside resort town and has the best beach in the region. Most of the accommodation in town can be found right along the beachfront and it provides the ideal destination for family fun. During the wet season, swimmers are protected by stinger nets.

Another favourite local activity is game of golf. Palm Meadows is the local course. There are two more great resort courses at nearby Port Douglas, and Cairns to the south, has several excellent layouts. The magnificent Great Barrier Reef lies just offshore and this means fantastic fishing and snorkelling and scuba diving activities.

Local tours and cruises to the reef and excellent fishing charters are available from both Cairns and Port Douglas. Both are regarded as world leaders in both sport's fishing and big game fishing with the outer reef dropoffs being home to the giant Black Marlin. Diving expeditions are available for a day or an extended trip to some of the worlds best dive sites. Port Douglas diving provides the opportunity to visit places like the Cod Hole and the Ribbon Reefs and Cairns Diving can take you on a day trip or deep into the Coral Sea to dive on remote and pristine coral reef systems.

Tours to the Atherton tableland or the world heritage listed Daintree rainforest will pick you up from your Palm Cove family accommodation and take you to visit these special places.

The town of Kuranda which is located on the Atherton table land can also be visited on one of the Skyrails gondola rides which is located only a short distance to the south of Palm Cove. Wildlife parks like Hartleys Crocodile exhibition are also located nearby. The Mossman Gorge is a fantastic destination for a family picnic and swimming in the crystal clear waters of this beautiful mountain river is most refreshing.

Your Palm Cove holiday can be filled with as many activities as you could possibly want like dining in the local restaurant and cafes or you can simply relax by the pool at you Palm Cove accommodation.

Palm Cove Dining - Restaurants and Cafes

Dining out in Palm Cove is one of the great pleasures of a holiday in this fantastic beachside resort town. Along the esplanade you will find many great options with a multitude of restaurants and resorts to choose from. Many of the resorts along this strip have alfresco A La carte restaurants in the front of their resorts and holidaymakers are welcomed wether they are staying in the reost or not. The tropical night air and the perfume of the Frangipanni and Melaleuka flowers fills the night air making it one of the most pleasant places you will ever dine out. Quality is excellent and the variety is fantastic.

Many people come to Palm Cove to celebrate their wedding and the dining houses here like to cater for a memorable reception. Si if you are planning you nuptials or just a relaxing vacation, Palm Cove is a great destination and the dining is fantastic.

Palm Cove Weddings

Receptions - Venues - Honeymoons

Palm Cove in North Queensland is a wonderful weddings destination. It has a superb climate and has all of the infrastructure that you will need to make your wedding a roaring success. There are a host of choices of locations for the ceremony itself. The beach is very popular with its views over the offshore islands and there are also some superb gardens and areas of rainforest. Many of the resorts offer a comprehensive wedding planning service and accommodation packages which makes it very attractive to bring in groups. Cairns is only a short distance away and you can fly in here from anywhere in Australia or from many overseas destinations. There are a multitude of shuttle services, taxis or limos available to get you to your chosen destination.

Several Palm Cove resorts have a range of facilities that will help with your planning. Kewarra Beach Resort & Spa is fabulous for your honeymoon with bures set in the jungle and really private swimming pools surrounded by rainforest. It is also located right on the beachfront. Mantra Amphora, Sea Temple resort and the Sebel Reef house also provide fantastic facility's and plenty of beachfront accommodation. Our local accommodation page has full details on all resorts in the area. All the other things you will need including hair and beauty treatments, Palm Cove wedding photography and marriage celebrants are readily available in the area. You should also see our Port Douglas weddings page if you are not yet sure exactly where, in the region, you want your wedding to be.

If you are thinking of a Palm Cove wedding, then give us a call, or drop us an email and one of our experienced staff will be able to assist you.

The End

Lightning Source UK Ltd.
Milton Keynes UK
UKHW012355030722
405312UK00002B/365